PEOPLE OF CHARACTER

Jackie Robinson

A Life of Determination

Written by Colleen Sexton
Illustrated by Tina Walski

BLASTOFF! READERS
4

BELLWETHER MEDIA • MINNEAPOLIS, MN

Note to Librarians, Teachers, and Parents:

Blastoff! Readers are carefully developed by literacy experts and combine standards-based content with developmentally-appropriate text.

Level 1 provides the most support through repetition of high-frequency words, light text, predictable sentence patterns, and strong visual support.

Level 2 offers early readers a bit more challenge through varied simple sentences, increased text load, and less repetition of high frequency words.

Level 3 advances early-fluent readers toward fluency through increased text and concept load, less reliance on visuals, longer sentences, and more literary language.

Level 4 builds reading stamina by providing more text per page, increased use of punctuation, greater variation in sentence patterns, and increasingly challenging vocabulary.

Level 5 encourages children to move from "learning to read" to "reading to learn" by providing even more text, varied writing styles, and less familiar topics.

Whichever book is right for your reader, Blastoff! Readers are the perfect books to build confidence and encourage a love of reading that will last a lifetime!

This edition first published in 2008 by Bellwether Media.

No part of this publication may be reproduced in whole or in part without written permission of the publisher. For information regarding permission, write to Bellwether Media Inc., Attention: Permissions Department, Post Office Box 1C, Minnetonka, MN 55345-9998.

Library of Congress Cataloging-in-Publication Data
Sexton, Colleen A., 1967–
  Jackie Robinson : a life of determination / by Colleen A. Sexton.
    p. cm. – (Blastoff! readers) (People of character)
Summary: "People of Character explores important character traits through the lives of famous historical figures. Jackie Robinson highlights how this great individual demonstrated determination during his life. Intended for grades three through six"—Provided by publisher.
  Includes bibliographical references and index.
  ISBN-13: 978-1-60014-089-1 (hardcover : alk. paper)
  ISBN-10: 1-60014-089-0 (hardcover : alk. paper)
  1. Robinson, Jackie, 1919–1972–Juvenile literature. 2. Baseball players–United States–Biography–Juvenile literature. 3. African American baseball players–Biography–Juvenile literature. I. Title.

  GV865.R6S49 2008
  796.357092–dc22
  [B]   2007014948

Contents

What if your dream
was to play baseball
in the major leagues?
What if you had the talent
but you weren't allowed
on a team because
of how you looked?
Jackie Robinson knew
how that felt. He was
an amazing **athlete**.
He was also black and
only whites could play
in the major leagues.

Jackie Robinson was born in 1919. His family lived in a mostly white area of Pasadena, California. Many of their neighbors didn't want to live near a black family.

Jackie

Some yelled **insults** at the Robinsons.
Some tried to make them move away.
But the Robinsons were **determined**
to stay!

Life was harder for blacks in some parts of the United States. They did not have the same rights as white people. Blacks couldn't live in the same neighborhoods as whites. They couldn't go to the same schools or libraries. Blacks couldn't even ride in elevators with whites. Keeping blacks separate from whites was called **segregation**. It was the law in some states.

Growing up, Jackie was good
at every sport he tried.
In college, Jackie was a star in
football, baseball, basketball,
and track. But sometimes he
was treated unfairly because of
his **race**. Some white students
wouldn't play with him.
When his team traveled, he
couldn't stay in the same hotels
as the white players. But Jackie
worked hard every day.
He was determined to be the
best athlete he could be.

In 1945, the Kansas City Monarchs
signed Jackie to play baseball.
The team had only black players.
Professional baseball was
segregated at the time.

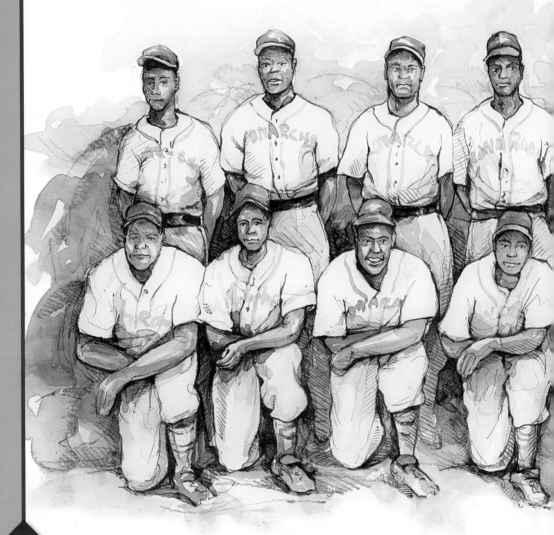

Whites played in the major leagues
and blacks played in the Negro
Leagues. Jackie played shortstop for the
Monarchs. He was also a talented hitter
and a quick runner.

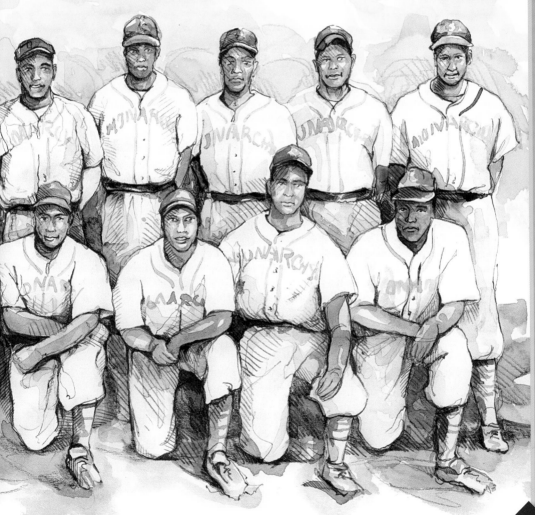

A man named Branch Rickey
noticed Jackie. Mr. Rickey was
president of a major league team
called the Brooklyn Dodgers.
He wanted talented athletes of
all races to play together.
In 1947, Mr. Rickey asked
Jackie to join the Dodgers.
Both men knew people would
treat Jackie badly. Jackie knew
being on the Dodgers would
be tough. Could he do it?

Jackie took the field with the Dodgers in 1947. The crowd yelled at him. Players on other teams shouted insults. Pitchers tried to hit him with the ball.

Some of his own teammates didn't want to play with him. It was hard, but Jackie was determined.
He wouldn't give up. He wouldn't show his anger. Instead, he would fight back by playing his best.

Soon everyone saw what Jackie could do on the field. He hit home runs and stole more bases than any other player.

Excited fans started to cheer for Jackie. He had 174 hits and scored 125 runs in his first season. He was even named **Rookie of the Year**. Jackie stayed with the Dodgers. In 1955 he helped the team win the World Series.

In 1962, Jackie became the first black player named to the Baseball Hall of Fame. By this time baseball fans of all races respected Jackie. He had opened the door to the major leagues for other black players. Jackie showed the world how determination can help make dreams come true.

Glossary

athlete—a person who plays sports

determination—deciding to do something and not giving up

insult—a rude and upsetting thing to say

professional—making money for doing a job

race—a group of people who have the same ancestors and share certain physical features such as skin color

Rookie of the Year—an award that goes to the best first-year player

segregation—the forced separation of groups of people according to their race, class, or gender

To Learn More

AT THE LIBRARY

Curtis, Gavin. *The Bat Boy and His Violin*. New York: Simon & Schuster, 1998.

Golenbock, Peter. *Teammates*. San Diego, Calif.: Harcourt Brace Jovanovich, 1990.

Lorbiecki, Marybeth. *Jackie's Bat*. New York: Simon & Schuster, 2006.

Ritter, Lawrence S. *Leagues Apart: The Men and Times of the Negro Baseball Leagues*. New York: Morrow Junior Books, 1995.

Uhlberg, Myron. *Dad, Jackie, and Me*. Atlanta, Ga.: Peachtree, 2005.

ON THE WEB

Learning more about Jackie Robinson is as easy as 1, 2, 3.

1. Go to www.factsurfer.com

2. Enter "Jackie Robinson" into search box.

3. Click the "Surf" button and you will see a list of related web sites.

With factsurfer.com, finding more information is just a click away.

Index